EAT YOUR WAY TO A HEALTHIER **PROSTATE**

Recipes for the man in your life with prostate cancer

John McLoughlin

Euromed Communications

ABOUT THE AUTHOR

John McLoughlin MS, FRCS Urol is a Consultant Urological Surgeon. He lives in Suffolk with his wife and four children.

ACKNOWLEDGEMENTS

Many thanks to Lynne and Betty, Jo Mayall, Dr. Sue Brown, Lorna Podbury, Mr Roger Giles and Dr. Claire Giles, Dr. Julia Hopkinson, Melissa Wesley and Dr. Sara Raton-Lunn for proofing the recipes. I would also like to thank Peter Jones for suggestions on the layout of this book and Elizabeth Tindall of the School of Hospitality and Tourism Studies, West Suffolk College, Bury St Edmunds for offering advice on many of the components of these recipes. Photography was by Peter and Adela Hayward.

Lastly, I am indebted to my little helpers in the garden and vegetable plot – Tom, Jack, Holly and Sam – without whom growing our fruit and veg would be much less fun.

Published by Euromed Communications Ltd

The Old Surgery, Liphook Road

Haslemere, Surrey GU27 1NL, UK

ISBN: 1 899015 50 7

Printed by Alden Press, Oxford, UK

This small book is for my poor wife, Lynne,
who puts up with me

Contents

Introduction — 1

The science behind the recipes — 3
How can diet improve your chances with prostate cancer? — 3
Evidence of links between diet and prostate cancer — 5

The basic components of your diet — 7

The Great British Diet — 9

Which foods are bad and which are good? — 13

Exercise, obesity, smoking and cardiovascular disease — 27

Applying the science — 31

Recipes

Dressings and Sauces
- Tomato Vinaigrette — 35
- Raspberry Vinaigrette — 35
- Spanish Orange Salad Dressing — 36
- Spanish Broccoli — 36
- Basic Tomato Sauce — 37
- Tomato and Basil Sauce — 37
- Basic Pizza Topping — 38
- Carrots with Orange Glaze — 38
- Broccoli & Carrots bathed in Orange Sauce — 39
- Tuna Dill Sandwich Spread — 40
- Hot Spinach Salad Dressing — 40

Soups
- Tom's Tomato Soup — 43
- Gazpacho — 44
- Brockley Tomato Soup — 44
- Fox Farm's Fishy Soup — 45
- Texan Tomato Soup — 46
- Potager Soup — 47
- Cool Garden Soup — 48
- Minestrone Soup — 49

Snacks and Salads
- Summer Vegetables — 51
- Stuffed Tomato Pots — 52
- Tomato Bread — 53
- Broccoli Salad — 54
- Marinated Carrot Salad — 54
- Salad Niçoise — 55
- Warm Cabbage — 55
- Tuna Salad — 56
- Red Cabbage and Green Apples — 57

Main Courses

Broccolied Colcannon 59
Sam's Chicken and Tomato Hot-Balls 60
Tuna Steaks with Orange and Grape Sauce 61
Baked Mackerel with Provençal Sauce 62
Broccoli and Mushroom Casserole 62
Broiled Salmon Fillet with Wine and Watercress Sauce 63
Jack's Tomato Caprese 64
Salmon Parcels 65
Courgette Fettuccine 66
Coq au Vin 67
Late Lucky Pasta 68
Ravioli à la Holly, 69
Koftas in Tomato Sauce 70
Crunchy Lemon Sardines with Rice 71

Desserts

Chilled Summer Fruit Cheesecake 73
Baked Raspberry Cheesecake 74
Melon with Summer Berries 75
Watermelon and Grape Compote 75
Guava Surprise 76
Boozy Strawberries 77
Vanilla Pudding 77

Drinks

Sam's Strawberry and Apple Smoothie 79
Raspberry and Pear Smoothie 79
Apple and Apricot Smoothie 80
Tofu Smoothie 80
Midsomer Fruit Juice 80
Strawberry and Banana Drink 81
Banana and Nutmeg 81
Raspberry Banana Tofu Ice Pops 81

Juiced Fruit and Vegetables

Juiced Fruit drinks 83
Juiced Vegetable drinks 84

Useful Contacts 85

Selected articles from recent medical literature 86

Notes 87

Man is what he eats
(Ludwig Feuerbach)

Introduction

We are literally what we eat. The inter-relationship between diet and prostate cancer comes up ever more frequently in my conversations with patients. This book is a result of their interest and their quest for information as to how **they** might positively influence their disease.

To the casual observer I would probably be the world's least likely advocate of a healthy diet. I have been a picky eater all my life. I disliked those bland vegetables forced on me during school dinners and hated tomatoes with a vengeance from a young age. So imagine my horror then when people started talking about the protective role of tomatoes and green-leafed vegetables against prostate cancer. However, mix those same humble vegetables into soups, snacks and recipes and they become food that even I can enjoy.

The aim of this book is not to make cooking a chore but rather to introduce you to foods that may be of value and offer a few practical suggestions of how they might be worked into your everyday meals. I hope you enjoy the book!

JMcL

The science behind the recipes

The prostate is a mischievous little gland. Cancer of the prostate affects 27,000 men per year in the UK and at any one time there are estimated to be around 100,000 men with the disease. The reasons why remain unclear but it seems likely that a number of factors conspire to produce a tumour. Genetic make-up certainly plays a part. External influences such as diet may also be important – with populations who eat a diet high in animal fat and low in soya produce, vegetables and fibre experiencing increased rates of prostate cancer.

Whilst there is not yet concrete proof that a better diet influences the development or course of any given prostate cancer, there is a growing body of medical opinion that a range of naturally occurring chemicals found in certain foods may be of benefit to such men. Diet may also affect the risk of dying of cardiovascular disease, another major killer in men who live with prostate cancer.

In my experience, most men will benefit psychologically from becoming 'master of their fate' by taking an interest in their diet and thereby in a part of their treatment programme.

How can diet improve your chances with prostate cancer?

There are three possible ways, by:

   i. influencing the actual prostate cancer

  ii. reducing cardiovascular disease in men living with prostate cancer

 iii. reducing obesity, and thereby influencing both of the above

  i. Prostate cancer does not develop completely by chance. It is really a multi-step process, that begins with an underlying genetic predisposition to the disease which is then modulated by complex interplay between factors that give rise to further genetic mutations that in turn prime a cell to become cancerous. At a cellular level this process can be seen to follow a recognised sequence of events – initiation, promotion and progression that develop into a clinical cancer.

    Our bodies metabolise fats and carbohydrates to produce energy by a process known as oxidation. This generates harmful molecules called free radicals that damage genetic material in cells, leading to tumour initiation.

    Healthy foods not only contain vitamins and minerals but also a range of beneficial chemicals such as antioxidants and phytochemicals – substances that fight cancer. Tomatoes, for example, contain protective antioxidants that form the first line of defense against the harmful effects of these free radicals.

If that genetic damage is not corrected the cell becomes potentially primed for tumour promotion. Saponins, found in whole grain foods, may be beneficial here.

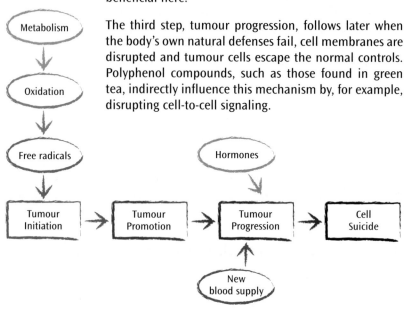

The third step, tumour progression, follows later when the body's own natural defenses fail, cell membranes are disrupted and tumour cells escape the normal controls. Polyphenol compounds, such as those found in green tea, indirectly influence this mechanism by, for example, disrupting cell-to-cell signaling.

As a tumour grows it needs a better blood supply. It grows one by sprouting tiny new blood vessels, a process called angiogenesis. This process is actually fundamental to normal wound healing throughout our life but is also central to cancer growth. Animal fats may cause harm by promoting angiogenesis.

The growth of prostate cancer is further modified by the balance of male sex hormones (androgens such as testosterone) and a number of subtle chemical reactions that change behaviour at a cellular level. The testes manufacture most of these hormones but some are produced in other areas of the body such as the adrenal gland and fat stores. Vegetables in the cabbage family contain hormone-like compounds that either mimic female hormones (oestrogens) or effectively mop up hormones, thus changing the balance in our favour.

Trace elements, such as selenium, may entice cancer cells to commit 'suicide' (a phenomenon known as apoptosis).

It is important to realise that when a variety of these foods are eaten together as part of a healthy balanced diet, their effects may provide a number of the above advantages at the same time.

ii. Cardiovascular disease causes hearts attacks and strokes and is the biggest killer of men in the UK. In men with prostate cancer it is still the most likely (or second most likely) cause of their death. A number of the foods that are good for the prostate also reduce the risk of heart disease. The key phrase is 'heart friendly is prostate friendly'.

iii. Obesity is a known risk factor for cardiovascular disease and is also thought to directly increase the risk of developing prostate cancer by as much as 20-30%.

Evidence of links between diet and prostate cancer

Studies that investigate the possible links between a population and disease (such as cancer) are called epidemiological studies. There are many study designs but those most frequently quoted with respect to diet and prostate cancer fall into 3 categories :

Migrant studies: These look at a population's disease rate before and after migration to a different country. Japanese men who migrated to America have been widely investigated in this way. Over time the prostate cancer rates of migrant Japanese approximated to that of American men (rising by 15-20 times of their original rates). As their genetics had not changed this would suggest that some external factor, such as diet was responsible. Soya produce was identified as a prime mover.

Cohort studies: In these, healthy populations are assessed for dietary factors at a baseline point and then later over a 10-15 year period. Such studies may involve people filling in food frequency questionnaires.

Case control studies: These compare the diet of men who develop prostate cancer with those who have not. The increased risk associated with red meat and high saturated fat intake was identified in this way.

Each design has its own potential strengths and weaknesses that limit their precise interpretation however. For example, one such case control study suggested that 18 servings of tomatoes per week could reduce prostate cancer risk by 35% whilst another identified no more than a weak link. For that reason it is safer to think of potential causal links as being in shades of grey rather than black and white.

In addition, there is some information from animal-based laboratory studies.

The basic components of your diet

Your food should ideally contain a blend of carbohydrates, protein, fat, fibre, vitamins and trace elements. We, as animals, were designed to forage around for nuts and berries and feed off the animals that lived (or died if we were lucky enough) in close proximity. Our bodies were never designed to cope with large intakes of refined sugars, processed foods and fats.

Carbohydrates

These are a source of energy. Dietary carbohydrates come from starches (also known as complex carbohydrates) which are found in potatoes and pasta, and from sugars (called simple carbohydrates) found in table sugar and breakfast cereals. We need carbohydrates but as animals we were never designed to consume the high quantity of processed sugar that we do. Unfortunately, too much of the sugar we consume is invisible, hidden in foods such as breakfast cereal or tinned produce. The fact that we eat so much sugar may explain the increasing number of diabetics in recent years.

Fats

It is worth spending a little time discussing fats, as they are probably the most important dietary influence on prostate cancer. Fats come from both animal and non-animal sources. They make food tasty and are a good source of energy. They carry essential fat-soluble vitamins A, D, E and K. Some fat intake is necessary in the diet but either eating too much or completely excluding them is harmful.

Fats are made up of two components : glycerin and fatty acids. It is the fatty acid components of fat that influence cancer. Fatty acids are divided into two main categories: **saturated** and **unsaturated** (further subdivided into mono and polyunsaturated). Saturated fat is solid at room temperature and is found in foods such as butter and lard. By contrast, unsaturated fat is pourable at room temperature and is found in vegetable oils.

Saturated and monounsaturated fatty acids are not really required in our diet as our bodies can synthesise them hence they are called 'non essential' fatty acids. However, other polyunsaturated fats cannot be made by our bodies and have to be eaten in food ('essential' fatty acids). There is yet another type of dietary fatty acid, the trans group. These are artificially made and utilised as food stabilisers and are linked to heart disease.

Two types of polyunsaturated fats frequently crop up in the debate on prostate cancer, namely the Omega 3 and the Omega 6 types. Omega 3 is found in rapeseed oil, soya beans, pumpkins, walnuts and oily fish (such as salmon, halibut, trout, tuna and herring) and are protective against prostate cancer. Omega 6 is found in olive oil, sunflower oil, mayonnaise and processed foods and is thought to have no effect on prostate cancer.

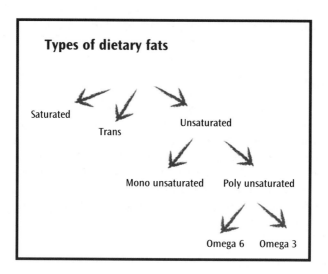

You should ensure that less than 25% of your total calorific intake is derived from fats and less than 10% of the total from saturated fat.

Proteins

Proteins are the building blocks for muscle and tissues. They are found in meats, poultry and fish. Soya beans are a good source of non-animal protein.

Fibre

This is the non-digestible part of food and is found in a range of grains, fruit and vegetables. It binds strongly to water, adding bulk to the stool and behaving as a colonic broom. Ideally you need about 25-30gm per day intake.

Vitamins and trace elements

These are silent workers, facilitating a wide range of invisible metabolic processes. They are found in a range of foods that form part of a healthy balanced diet. A number of them are thought to benefit prostate cancer.

The Great British Diet

As a nation, our diet has changed over the last 50 years. In general we are becoming healthier eaters!

Fats and carbohydrates

Between the 1950s and 1970s there was a decline in the proportion of food energy provided from carbohydrates and a corresponding rise in that provided by fats. This trend has stabilised since the mid 70s and over the last 25 years our total intake of fat has fallen progressively. The proportion of animal-based saturated fats in the diet has also declined, with low-fat spreads and vegetable oils replacing butter, margarine and lard. Polyunsaturated and monounsaturated fats are on the increase, as unfortunately are the 'trans' fats (often hidden in processed foods, cakes, etc). Total milk consumption has fallen whilst the actual proportion of skimmed milk consumed has risen.

In general terms we tend to take in more energy per day now than in the 70s. In the United States a similar increase in caloric intake occurred over the same period. However, as a nation, the US has now become obsessed with 'low fat' foods, often at the expense of high hidden salt and sugar content. It is estimated that about one third of all calories consumed in the US are derived from so-called non-nutritional foods, such as refined sugars, etc.

It is also worth mentioning water. When we drink water nowadays we often consume sugar-rich water, such as that found in beverages.

Protein

Our intake of beef, lamb, bacon, ham and pork rose sharply in the 1950s but has steadily declined ever since. However, the amount of meat-based produce hidden in pre-prepared foods has risen. Our average consumption of cooked and red meat is about 90gm/day (cooked weight) – roughly equivalent to 8-10 servings per week. Men continue to eat more meat produce than women.

Poultry consumption has increased markedly and is now equal to that of beef, lamb and pork combined! Fish consumption has fallen slightly over the last 50 years whereas soya-based protein, whilst rising progressively, still only amounts to a small proportion of our total national protein intake.

Bread and cereals

Bread consumption has halved whereas cereals have risen slightly (this sounds encouraging but remember a lot of 'healthy' cereals have large quantities of hidden sugar).

Fruit and vegetables

Our fruit and vegetable intake has risen by 30% and 50% respectively. Leafy salad produce accounts for most of this increase whilst the protective brassicas, peas and beans in our diet have fallen by two thirds. Two thirds of the fruit and veg we eat are fresh.

Trace elements

Our consumption of calcium has dropped since the 1960s. Selenium intake is stable but still low (probably only about 30-60mcg/day compared to an optimal 200mcg/day), especially in comparison to our American counterparts.

quod me nutrit me destruit
(that which feeds me destroys me)

Which foods are bad and which are good?

The bad

Dietary (saturated) animal fat

There is a phrase 'quod me nutrit me destruit' which roughly translates to 'that which feeds me destroys me'. This is certainly true of the fat content of your diet. The harmful effect of saturated animal fat on prostate cancer is well known. There is a direct relationship between the amount of dietary fat intake and risk of developing prostate cancer. The average western diet contains 30% animal fat-reducing this to even 20% may be beneficial although you should aim to reduce it to 10%.

Saturated fats are either obvious and visible (eg. the rind on a piece of bacon) or invisible (embedded within a piece of red meat, biscuits or a piece of cake). Every effort should be made to reduce saturated fat consumption. Where animal protein is consumed it should preferably be of either fish or poultry (skinned) origin. Meat and milk intake should be restricted or alternatively be replaced by a non-animal protein such as soya or by fish. Fish also provides a good source of vitamins A and D. With the exception of tuna, most tinned fish is every bit as good as fresh fish.

Saturated fats probably exert their influence by either altering sex hormone production or by adjusting the level of chemicals that bind to these hormones, thereby altering their internal balance. They also work through the actions of one of their components called arachidonic acid, or by intermediate chemicals known as prostaglandins that act on the tiny new blood vessels associated with tumour growth.

Fat sources	
Harmful fats	**Protective fats**
Margarine	Nuts and seeds
Cakes, crisps and biscuits	Olive oil
Animal fats	Avocados
High dairy fat	Fish oils

Red meat

Red meats include beef, lamb, pork and processed meat in products such as sausages, hamburgers or other foods.

Controlled studies of men who eat large quantities of red meat indicate that they may have double the risk of developing prostate cancer compared to those with low consumption. One of the problems with such studies is that red meat intake has a close relationship to saturated fat intake, another potential 'agent provocateur' so it may not be an independent risk factor. Nevertheless, it seems good advice to reduce your consumption of red meat.

Dairy produce

High-fat dairy produce is an obvious source of saturated animal fat. If possible, use low-fat milk or try soya-based substitutes (much more palatable when disguised in drinks and puddings).

The good

Most of the 'good group' belong to the plant world, although the benefits of natural fish oils cannot be overlooked. Fruit and vegetables not only supply us with essential vitamins and minerals, but also are rich in phytochemicals (plant-derived natural hormone-like substances that mimic female hormones) and protective antioxidants. Many of the phytochemicals are associated with strong colours or powerful flavours.

Tomatoes

Tomatoes owe their red colour to natural pigments called lycopenes. Lycopenes have powerful antioxidant properties capable of blocking the detrimental effects of free radicals on genetic material. Tomatoes are also a good source of other antioxidants such as vitamins C and E.

Humans cannot make lycopenes and rely upon dietary consumption where they act as precursors of vitamin A. Lycopenes persist in the body for several days after ingestion so when taken regularly as part of a diet they remain chemically active, even when the odd day is missed. The average intake in the UK is only 1mg/ day, compared to 5mg/day in the North America. It has been suggested that 8mg/day is the optimal intake. In real terms you should aim to eat 10 or more servings of tomato produce per week.

Tomatoes account for about 90% of the lycopenes in the average man's diet

But not all tomato produce are born equal...

The actual lycopene content of tomato-based produce varies a lot depending upon how it is processed. Careful inspection of a number of tomato-based products will also alert you to their lycopene content, as illustrated below:

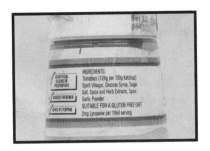

Lycopene content displayed on a tomato ketchup bottle

Processed tomato produce may, however, contain added sugar and salt.

Cooking tomatoes in olive oil increases the amount of lycopene available for absorption by the gut, although cooking tomatoes may reduce vitamin C and flavenoid content. The best way to enjoy tomatoes is to eat both raw and cooked produce. In the opinion of the author, the best of these happen to be British grown tomatoes.

Lycopenes form part of larger group of red, yellow and orange plant pigments collectively known as carotenoids, all of which have antioxidant properties. They also influence cell-to-cell communications and receptor action. Carotenoids exist naturally in the plant kingdom and protect the plant DNA from the harmful effects of ionising ultraviolet light. They are found in a wide range of coloured fruit and vegetables such as carrots, strawberries, lychees and red watermelon. For the average man, however, tomatoes remain the largest source of dietary carotenoid.

Relative amounts of biologically active lycopene from different types of tomato produce	
Fresh tomatoes	Moderate
Cooked tomatoes	Higher
Tomato sauce	Very high
Tomato purée	Very high
Tomato ketchup	High
Canned pizza sauce	High

In gardening circles 'super-carrots' are emerging, bred for their increased carotenoid content. One such example is a carrot variety called 'Health master', which is claimed to provide an extra 35% of beta-carotene.

A lesser-known group of plant pigments are the flavanoids (also referred to as bioflavanoids) which impart their green, blue, purple and sometimes red colour to fruit and vegetables. This group acts in synergism with vitamin C and exerts both anti-oxidant and phytochemical actions. Green teas are also a good source (see below).

Soya bean produce

The potential medicinal importance of the soya bean was recognised as far back as 2838 BC when the Chinese emperor Sheng-nung designated it as one of his 'sacred crops'.

Soya beans contain natural compounds called isoflavones that, when acted upon by intestinal bacteria, convert to phytochemicals that mimic female hormones. These weak, naturally occurring hormones act by affecting new blood vessel formation around tumours and by promoting cancer cell suicide. The best known is Genestein, although others such as Equol and Daidzein are also found in abundance in soya produce. Genestein may exert its effects by a variety of different actions including enzymic activity, angiogenesis and promoting cancer cell suicide. Soya produce is also a good source of Omega 3 fatty acids and vitamin D.

A high intake of dietary isoflavones may explain the observation that populations of Japanese men living in Japan have reduced prostate cancer rates. When these groups migrate to Western countries and adopt Western diets that are low in soya produce they experience Western rates of prostate cancer. Most authors recommend a daily intake of 20-40 grams of soya produce as optimal. By using a little imagination you can easily increase your daily intake. For instance try soya milk with your breakfast cereal or in fruit smoothie drinks or alternatively add fresh green soya beans to salads, or cooked beans to chilli recipes. Soya flour can be used in part as a flour substitute when baking cakes.

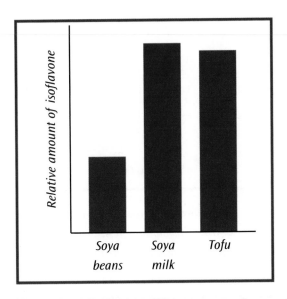

The relative amount of isoflavones in different types of soya produce varies widely – as with tomato produce – with tofu, soya flour and soya milk having the highest relative values.

Soya is also a good source of non-animal protein and fibre and helps to control cholesterol levels.

Cruciferous vegetables

The cruciferous group belongs to the cabbage family of vegetables and are identified by their 4-leaved flowers. They contain a number of sulphur-based phytochemical precursors that give this group their typical cabbage-like taste and are degraded by prolonged cooking.

Cabbages owe their characteristic taste, and their health benefits, to their sulphur content

Our intake of cauliflower, along with other members of the cruciferous family of vegetables, has fallen in recent years but it remains a useful source of dietary phytochemicals

The cabbage (cruciferous) family of vegetables	
Broccoli	Turnips
Brussels sprouts	Turnip green
Cabbage	Radishes
Cauliflower	Swiss chard
Collard greens	Horseradish
Watercress	Beet greens
Kohlrabi	

They are also rich in Glutathione-S-transferase (GST), an enzyme involved in the antioxidant process that inactivates carcinogens. This enzyme is interesting as it is abundant in normal prostatic tissue but absent in a high proportion of cancerous prostates. Cruciferous vegetables are a good source of protective phytochemicals called Sulphorophane and Indole-3-carbinol (a by-product of the GST enzyme).

Some refer to this group of vegetables as the 'crucial cruciferous' and others as the 'cruciferous crusaders'.

The actual quantity of phyto-oestrogens varies even among different varieties of a given vegetable. Take broccoli for example, which is known to be high in phytochemicals. The calabrese-type broccoli known as 'Trixie' is popular with gardeners because of its tolerance to the plant disease, clubroot. 'Trixie' has a much higher content of phytochemical precursors relative to other broccoli – so

Dietary sources of phytochemicals	
Herbs and seasoning	garlic, parsley
Grains	soya bean, wheat, rice
Cruciferous vegetables	cabbage, broccoli, spinach
Other vegetables	carrots, legumes
Fruits	dates, pomegranates, cherries, apples
Drinks	coffee, red wine

high that a new 'super broccoli' has been cross-bred commercially in an effort to utilise this property. The first such seeds available for the amateur gardener will not be available for a few years yet but the future trend is likely to be one of many such designer-bred plants rich in a particular chemical. Fresh sprouting broccoli has probably the highest content of phytochemical of all.

Quercetin

This is found in onions (which gives onion skins their lovely brown colour), raspberries, strawberries, red wine and broccoli. It acts as an antioxidant, has hormone-like properties and also exerts activity against a protein called Bc12 that promotes cancer cell turnover and division. Red onions also contain anthocyanins that are antioxidants. A recent Australian study has confirmed the protective role of onions.

Both onions and garlic have strong flavours associated with a sulphur-based chemical called allicin, which also lowers blood cholesterol levels.

*Onions contain quercetin, a powerful antioxidant
and allicin, a phytochemical precursor*

Soft fruits

Any gardener will know the term 'soft fruit' refers to lovely summer produce such as raspberries, strawberries, blackberries and blackcurrants, etc. Such fruit contain a range of goodies including the antioxidants vitamin C, anthocyanin and carotenoids, courtesy of their rich colouring. They are also an excellent source of dietary fibre and the phytochemical, ellargic acid.

Vitamin C

Vitamin C has antioxidant properties and is also important for tissue healing. It is found in a wide range of fruit and vegetables, especially citrus fruits. It is water soluble and rapidly excreted in the urine necessitating a regular intake.

Vitamin D

The metabolically active form of vitamin D is known as calciferol and plays a central role in calcium and bone metabolism. Experimental data from animal studies have found vitamin D receptors on prostate cancer cells that can alter tumour growth. Some evidence from epidemiological cohort studies showed that men who have lower levels of vitamin D are more likely to develop prostate cancer. Despite this, rather than trying to supplement vitamin D in your diet you would do better to eat more fructose-rich fruit, which in turn will boost your vitamin D levels and provides a non-fat source of energy.

Fructose

Fructose is the natural sugar found in fruit. It is a useful, non-fat source of energy, the same fruits providing a good source of vitamin C. It also enhances vitamin D formation and can only be of help, indeed one study recently showed that eating more than 70g per day can reduce prostate cancer risk.

Apples are good for you. They contain vitamin C, fructose and fibre

Selenium and vitamin E

Both appear to have antioxidant properties and have the ability to induce cancer 'cell suicide'. Selenium also has an indirect effect as it is essential to the Glutathione-S-transferase antioxidant enzyme system described above.

Selenium is found in lentils, broccoli, nuts and oily fish but is present in relatively low quantities in our soil and consequently in most other British vegetables. This deficit appears to be a leftover from the last ice age, when the glaciers washed selenium out of the topsoil of Great Britain and Northern Europe! The average daily intake is now around only 30-60mcg/day whereas the optimal daily intake is thought to be 200mcg/day. Selenium is probably one of the few dietary supplements that can be advocated in tablet form although any benefits are probably only going to be derived if you were deficient in the first place!

Vitamin E is fat-soluble and found in fish oils and nuts. It remains in the body for long periods of time and should not be taken to excess over a long period. One epidemiological study suggested that a daily vitamin E supplement might reduce the prostate cancer risk by 32%. However such supplements are not generally recommended if you have a healthy diet. If you are a smoker (why are you a smoker?) supplements may apparently be of greater value.

There is currently a large study of over 30,000 men to assess the relative protection offered by Selenium and vitamin E, either alone or in combination, against prostate cancer (the SELECT study). It will be some years before the outcome is known.

Broccoli is a true 'cruciferous crusader'. It is a good source
of selenium and has a high phytochemical content.

Strawberries contain vitamin C, ellargic acid and carotenoids

Green tea

Green tea contains polyphenols (a member of the flavanoid group of nutrients) the best known of which are the catechin group. It is made from the leaves of *Camellia sinensis*, a tea plant that is commonly consumed in China and Japan and is made by lightly steaming and drying the tea leaves. This process allows the polyphenols to remain intact in contrast to the brewing process that produces the traditional brown tea westerners drink and in doing so destroys these useful products.

Polyphenols act against the enzymes urokinase and ornithine decarboxylase, which alter cell membranes and protein metabolism in human cancer cells. They may also influence 5-alpha reductase, an enzyme intimately involved in prostatic metabolism, producing cell suicide, which indirectly affects cancer progression.

Zinc

Zinc is an essential trace element that is present in high concentrations in the healthy prostate. Its exact role is unclear but is thought to be protective, possibly acting as an antioxidant. It is found in vegetables, especially peas.

Blackcurrants are a surprisingly good source of fibre.
They also contain ellargic acid and vitamin C

Melons are a source of vitamin C, lycopenes and fibre

Fibre

Do not ignore your fibre intake! Fibre (commonly called roughage) is of two types:

- **Soluble fibre**, which is found in oats, vegetables, fruit and beans, regulates the bowels and also cholesterol and blood sugar levels. High soluble fibre intake can make you very flatulent!

- **Insoluble fibre** is found in brown rice and wholemeal bread and is recognised as a good 'colonic broom'. This type of fibre also contains precursor chemicals that, when attacked by intestinal bacteria, is converted to lignans (eg. enterolactone) which have both oestrogenic and hormone-binding properties. Linseed (also known as flaxseed) is the best known and the widest researched lignan source.

   Whole grain foods also contain other goodies, such as saponins, which interfere with cancer cell turnover.

You need a minimum of about 18-20g fibre / day. Both types of dietary fibre are important and you should ideally aim for 60 insoluble / 40 soluble fibre ratio in your diet. Most of us in the West consume too high a proportion of the soluble type.

Dietary vegetable oil

Not all fats are bad, indeed those containing Omega 3 compounds, found in oily fish, vegetable oil and soya beans, are protective. Mono-unsaturated fats like olive oil and peanut oil probably have little effect but as they tend to be eaten in the Mediterranean diet alongside tomatoes they are useful. Similarly polyunsaturated fat products are not detrimental in moderate amounts and serve as useful alternatives to foods such as butter or lard.

Alcohol

It has been suggested that alcohol, by increasing urine output, may reduce the effects of some water-soluble antioxidants such as vitamin C. In reality it probably has little or no effect. Indeed resveratrol is found in red grapes, grape juice and red wine and may have antioxidant or anti-angiogenic properties. Red wine also contains polyphenols and quercetin.

Raspberries are full of ellargic acid and vitamin C

Red and yellow peppers provide a rich source of carotenoids

The questionable

Calcium

It had previously been suggested that dietary calcium might in some way be detrimental for men with prostate cancer. There is a rationale for this theory – calcium metabolism is linked with that of vitamin D (and its metabolically active form, calcitrol). However a recent American study has shown that calcium intake within the recommended daily allowance is not associated with any increased risk. This is clearly good news as some calcium intake is needed for good health, strong bones and teeth. The typical dietary sources of calcium include milk, cheese and eggs.

Vitamin A

Most studies show that vitamin A has little or no effect on prostate cancer. In excessive doses vitamin A may be detrimental – indeed, in very high doses it can be toxic as it is fat-soluble so your body cannot excrete vitamin A easily. Again, the value of a balanced diet should be emphasised.

The bad	The good	The questionable
Animal fat	Antioxidants	High vitamin A intake
High milk intake	Phytochemicals	High calcium intake
	Isoflavones	
	Vegetable oils	
	Fish oils	
	vitamin D	
	Quercetin	
	Fructose	

Exercise, obesity, smoking and cardiovascular disease

Obesity

Obese men appear to have an increased risk of developing prostate cancer, possibly by as much as 20-30%. In the UK 44% of men are classified as overweight and 15% as obese.

You can calculate whether or not you have a problem by using a Body Mass Index (BMI) calculation, based on your weight and height. You should aim for a BMI of between 20-25. Work out yours by the following equation:

Calculate your BMI

$$\frac{\text{weight (kilograms)}}{\text{height (metres)} \times \text{height (metres)}} \quad \text{or} \quad \frac{\text{weight (pounds)}}{\text{height (inches)} \times \text{height (inches)}} \times 704$$

As a man, a simpler way for you to assess if your weight is about right is to make a rough comparison of your waist measurement (largest circumference when standing) to that of your hips (largest circumference measurement around your buttock area) – if your waist measurement is greater than your hip measurement, you are probably too heavy.

There may be a number of reasons why men who are overweight are more likely to develop prostate cancer. For example, fat deposits are sites of non-testicular steroidal hormone conversion; peroxidised fat deposits may promote cancer growth; men who are overweight appear to have impaired macrophage function (which act as immune scavengers) or increased insulin resistance. It is said that for men with a BMI of between 30-35 the risk of developing prostate cancer is increased by 20%, whilst those with a BMI of over 35 the increase is about 30%.

It is also worth keeping your weight down as it may reduce your chances of developing cardiovascular disease.

Exercise

Exercise is good for you! It produces a sense of well being, it helps you sleep better, keeps your weight down and is beneficial to your heart.

Cardiovascular disease

Cardiovascular disease causes heart attacks and strokes, which are the commonest causes of death for men in the UK. This is worth remembering, as even if you have prostate cancer, cardiovascular disease will still be either the most likely, or second most likely, risk of your dying prematurely.

Men in the UK live on average 5 years less than women, with 20% of men dying prematurely from cardiovascular disease. Obesity, high blood pressure, smoking, high cholesterol levels and lack of exercise all contribute to this figure.

You should become familiar with your 'lipid profile'. You will probably already have heard of cholesterol, but its predictive value in terms of assessing who is at risk of a heart attack is limited and most doctors now recognise that other lipid components are just as important. Low-density lipoproteins (known as 'LDL') are harmful and their level should be less than 4mmol/l. High-density lipoproteins ('HDL') are protective and should be higher than 1.5mmol/l. Triglycerides shouldn't worry you unless your fasting levels are higher than 1.5 mmol/l.

Lipid profiles	
	Ideal values
Cholesterol	less than 5.2mmol/l
Low density lipoprotein (LDL)	less than 4mmol/l
High density lipoprotein (HDL)	over 1.5mmol/l
Triglycerides	less than 1.5mmol/l

Remember that a diet low in saturated animal fats and meat is good for both your heart and prostate. Soya produce, for example, is a good source of non-animal protein, a good source of fibre and will also help lower your cholesterol. What is heart friendly is prostate friendly.

Smoking

It is sad reflection of our health as a nation that, even in the third millennium, 28% of men still smoke tobacco. It makes no sense to continue smoking if you are trying to beat prostate cancer. Whilst there is no clear link between smoking and prostatic malignancy as such, there are a whole host of diseases linked with smoking that will potentially shorten your life, including cardiovascular disease, lung, bladder and oral cancer, chronic lung disease and peptic ulceration. A life-long male smoker has only a 43% chance of reaching 73 years of age compared to a 78% chance for a non-smoker.

Applying the science

The basic rules

It is important to enjoy your food. It should not become a chore to eat. The natural chemicals in these foods work best when in combination, such as would be found in a healthy balanced diet, rather than by artificial nutritional supplements. Avoid where possible 'magic bullet' supplements in tablet form.

- Eat plenty of fruit and vegetables – at least 5 portions a day. Try 'juicing' fruit and vegetables to increase your consumption. Some juiced vegetables can be added to stews or sauces. Eat plenty of tomatoes. Cooked or processed tomato produce is better still.

How big is a portion when aiming for 5 portions per day?

1 portion =
- 2 tablespoonfuls of vegetable
- a handful of berries or grapes
- a fruit such as an apple, banana or orange
- a big slice of a large fruit (eg. melon) or 2 small whole fruit (eg. satsumas)

(fruit juice only counts as a ½ portion no matter how much you drink!)

It is surprisingly easy to get a good selection of fresh, pre-packed vegetables in supermarkets, even if you are too busy to shop around for these individually. Below are a couple of examples of 'off the shelf' produce from a popular supermarket chain.

Examples of pre-packed vegetable mixes

> ### Tips on preparing fruit and vegetables
>
> - Use larger pieces so as to reduce wash-out effect of cooking
> - Cook vegetables in their skins (for example, vitamin C is found just under the skin of potatoes)
> - Steam cook vegetables where possible. When cooking in water, try to reduce the amount of water in which they are prepared (some nutrients are water-soluble)
> - Cook until tender but still crisp, not overdone

- Cut down animal fats as much as possible. Use skinless poultry, fish (especially oily fish rich in Omega 3 fats) or soya produce to replace red meat. Reduce your weekly meat intake to less than 90 gm / week. Where you eat meat cut off excess fat. Spread butter and margarine thinly on bread and scrape off any excess. Try to bake, steam, poach or grill food rather than fry it. Ensure that less than 25% of your calories are derived from fat and less than 10 % from saturated fat.

- Reduce your consumption of red meat where possible. Eat poultry, fish and soya produce as an alternative. Remember heart friendly is prostate friendly.

- Reduce your intake of milk and other dairy foods, especially full-fat produce.

- Get into a regular exercise regime. Try for at least 10 minutes of swimming or 20 minutes walking, riding a bike or even mowing the lawn per day.

- Keep your height / weight ratio optimal and maintain your BMI in the range 20-25.

- Eat more unprocessed foods, whole grains and wholemeal bread. Aim for 30gm fibre intake per day.

- Drink red wine in moderation.

- Stop smoking. This makes sense.

- Make sure you keep your cholesterol and lipid profiles optimal.

- The content and nutritional value of most food is now clearly displayed on the packaging. Teach yourself to read the composition labels on the side of jars, cans or packets. You will often be surprised by their hidden saturated fat content. The amount of sugar is also of interest – if you value your teeth. A lot of low fat foods are actually high in sugar – especially cereals and 'healthy' yogurts and drinks.

NUTRITION INFORMATION	Per 37.5g Serving	Per 100g Serving
Energy	540kJ/ 128kcal	1440kJ/ 340kcal
Protein	4.2g	11.2g
Carbohydrate	25.4g	67.6g
(of which sugars)	(1.8g)	(4.7g)
Fat	1.0g	2.7g
(of which saturates)	(0.2g)	(0.6g)
Fibre	3.9g	10.5g
(of which soluble)	(1.2g)	(3.2g)
(of which insoluble)	(2.7g)	(7.3g)
Sodium	0.10g	0.27g

Dressings and Sauces

TOMATO VINAIGRETTE

2 large tomatoes   **Serves 4**
1 small clove of garlic, peeled
15ml / 1 tablespoon of red wine vinegar
15ml / 1 tablespoon of olive oil
salt and freshly ground pepper
1 tablespoon of fresh basil for the garnish

1. Place all ingredients, except basil, in a blender.
2. Pass the mix through a sieve to extract the tomato skins and seeds.
3. Store in a fridge until required.
4. Garnish with basil prior to serving.

RASPBERRY VINAIGRETTE

A simple addition that will liven up any salad.

a handful of fresh raspberries   **Serves 4**
50ml / 2 fl oz of raspberry vinegar
50ml / 2 fl oz of extra virgin olive oil
1 teaspoon of sugar in 100ml / 4 fl oz of water
1 tablespoon of mixed dried herbs
a pinch of salt
½ teaspoon of fresh ground black pepper
1 clove of garlic, crushed

1. Blend all the ingredients until smooth.
2. Leaving the dressing in a fridge for at least an hour before serving.

SPANISH ORANGE SALAD DRESSING

An elegant dressing, rich in Vitamin C.

6 medium oranges   **Serves 4**

200g / 7oz fresh strawberries

1 teaspoon sugar

75ml / 5 tablespoons of extra virgin oil

mint leaves to garnish

freshly ground black pepper

1. Prepare the segments of orange by using a serrated knife and cutting away the pith and membranes.
2. Cut the strawberries into chunks.
3. Arrange the segments on a plate, sprinkle with sugar and spoon over the orange juice.
4. Drizzle the oil over the segments and garnish with halved strawberries and mint leaves.
5. Sprinkle with ground pepper.

SPANISH BROCCOLI

225g / 8oz broccoli   **Serves 4**

225g / 8oz carrots

45ml / 3 tablespoons of extra virgin olive oil

1 clove of garlic, crushed

½ teaspoon of smoked paprika

1. Steam the broccoli and carrots in a pan until tender, then transfer to a plate to keep warm.
2. Heat olive oil and sauté the crushed garlic until golden, then add the smoked paprika.
3. When all the paprika has been covered with the oil, add the broccoli and carrots.
4. Season with salt.
5. Serve immediately.

BASIC TOMATO SAUCE

This basic sauce is great with pasta-based foods.

30ml / 2 tablespoons of olive oil   **Serves 4**
2 large onions, finely chopped
2 cloves of garlic, chopped
800g / 1¾ lb of canned tomatoes in natural juice
basil and oregano seasoning (or use a herb of your choice)
60ml / 4 tablespoons of tomato puree

1. Sauté the onions and garlic in olive oil over gentle heat until the onion is transparent.
2. Chop the tomatoes and add to onions and garlic, along with juice from the tomatoes.
3. Add tomato puree and herbs.
4. Mix well and simmer gently for about 10 minutes.

TOMATO AND BASIL SAUCE

A variation of the above sauce.

115g / 4oz of chopped basil   **Serves 4**
2 garlic cloves, chopped
2 large tomatoes, peeled
60ml / 4 tablespoons of olive oil

1. Mix all the ingredients about an hour before they are required.
2. Store in a fridge until served.

BASIC PIZZA TOPPING

Makes enough to cover 1 large or 2 small pizza bases.

175g / 6oz tomato puree
350ml / 7 fl oz of water
75ml / 5 tablespoons of extra virgin olive oil
2 tablespoons of mixed herbs
2 cloves of garlic, crushed
salt and freshly ground pepper to taste

1. Mix the tomato puree, water and olive oil. It doesn't need cooking!
2. Add garlic and herbs and allow to stand for several hours prior to serving.
3. Spread on pizza base.

CARROTS WITH ORANGE GLAZE

6 carrots, peeled and cut into long strips   **Serves 6**
15ml / 1 tablespoon of olive oil
30ml / 2 tablespoons of water
3 teaspoons of sugar
1 teaspoon of cornflour
85ml / 6 tablespoons of fresh orange juice
orange slices for garnish

1. Boil the carrots until tender, then drain and transfer carrots to a shallow baking dish.
2. To make the glaze, mix the olive oil and water in a small saucepan.
3. In a separate small container, mix sugar and cornflour.
4. Little by little, stir in the cornflour / sugar mix into olive oil / water mixture in a saucepan. Put the saucepan on low heat, gradually stirring in orange juice.
5. Heat until the mixture thickens and bubbles gently, stirring constantly.
6. Pour glaze evenly over carrots.
7. Bake at 180°C (350°F / Gas Mark 4) for 15 minutes.
8. Garnish with twisted halves of orange slices.
9. Serve immediately.

BROCCOLI & CARROTS BATHED IN ORANGE SAUCE

225g / 8oz broccoli **Serves 4 – 6**
225g / 8oz carrots
120ml / 4 fl oz of chicken stock
120ml / 4 fl oz of freshly squeezed orange juice
2 teaspoons of cornflour
1 onion, sliced
1 bay leaf
½ teaspoon of sugar
1 small orange

1. Steam the broccoli and carrots until tender, then transfer to a plate to keep warm.
2. Stir together the chicken stock and orange juice in a pan.
3. Add cornflour to mix and stir until it dissolves.
4. Add onions, bay leaf, and sugar, bringing mixture to the boil.
5. Reduce heat and simmer until sauce begins to thicken and bubble.
6. Cook for a further minute.
7. Add the sliced orange, broccoli and carrots to the mix, so as to coat with the sauce.
8. Serve immediately.

TUNA DILL SANDWICH SPREAD

1 small ripe tomato **Serves 2**
185g / 6½oz of tuna canned in brine
½ – 1 teaspoon of fresh dill
1 tablespoon of fresh parsley
2.5ml / ½ tablespoon of olive oil
1 small spring onion
½ cucumber, cut into 2.5cm / 1 inch lengths
3 medium mushrooms, chopped coarsely
1ml / ⅛ teaspoon of red wine vinegar

1. Drain the brine from the tuna.
2. Core out the tomato leaving only the shell, discard the pips.
3. Chop all ingredients until you obtain a thick mixture.
4. Add the olive oil and red wine vinegar now.
5. Season with salt and freshly ground pepper taste.
6. Serve immediately.

HOT SPINACH SALAD DRESSING

275g / 10oz spinach **Serves 6**
1 red onion, thinly sliced
175g / 6oz pine nut kernels
200g / 7oz crumbled blue cheese
300ml / ½ pint of balsamic vinegar
1 clove garlic crushed
15ml / 3 teaspoons of black treacle
200ml / 7 fl oz of olive oil

1. Arrange the spinach, red onion slices, blue cheese and pine kernels in a salad bowl.
2. In a small saucepan, warm the garlic in the olive oil over a gentle heat.
3. Add black treacle and vinegar.
4. Turn up the heat but do not allow to the boil, whisking continually.
5. Remove from heat and cool dressing until just warm. Pour into a screw-top jar and shake.
6. Pour over the spinach mixture.
7. Season with freshly ground black pepper and serve immediately.

Soups

TOM'S TOMATO SOUP

This is a favourite of my son, Tom. It is quite filling
which probably explains why he never finishes
the rest of his meal!

2 garlic cloves, crushed   **Serves 4**

15ml / 1 tablespoon of olive oil

400g / 14oz can of tomatoes, chopped

30ml / 2 tablespoons of tomato puree

1 teaspoon of light brown sugar

*1 tablespoon of cornflour, dissolved in 45 ml / 3 tablespoons of water to make
a cornflour paste*

2 celery sticks, chopped

2 vegetable stock cubes, dissolved in 450 ml / ¾ pint of boiling water

1 large onion, chopped

1 teaspoon of dried mixed herbs

60ml / 4 tablespoons of very low fat crème fraîche

a sprig of basil to garnish

1. Place the celery, onion and garlic in a pan with olive oil and soften over a gentle heat.
2. Add the tomatoes, tomato puree, sugar and stock and bring to the boil. Simmer for about 15 minutes.
3. Pour the mix into a blender and blend until you achieve a soft runny consistency, then pass it through a sieve to remove the tomato seeds.
4. Pour the soup back into a saucepan and add the cornflour paste.
5. Heat gently, stirring whilst the soup thickens.
6. Season with salt and pepper.
7. Garnish with basil and a dollop of crème fraîche.
8. Serve immediately. Best served piping hot.

GAZPACHO

1 green pepper, halved and deseeded   **Serves 4**
⅓ cucumber, cut into small pieces
500g / 1¼ lb of peeled and quartered tinned tomatoes
1 garlic clove, crushed
30ml/ 2 tablespoons of extra virgin olive oil
1 bunch of fresh spring onions, roughly chopped into small pieces
½ teaspoon of cumin
finely chopped cucumber can be added to garnish if desired

1. Mix all the ingredients except the spring onions.
2. Puree the mixture and season with salt and ½ teaspoon of cumin.
3. Store in fridge until ready to use.
4. Sprinkle with finely chopped onions just prior to serving.

BROCKLEY TOMATO SOUP

We tried this for the first time the year that we
started growing our own home-grown tomatoes.
The fresher the ingredients the better the taste.

½ medium sized onion, diced   **Serves 4 – 6**
30ml / 2 tablespoons of extra virgin olive oil
1 clove of garlic, crushed
600ml / 1 pint of vegetable stock
1 large (or 2 small) ripe tomato, cut into small pieces
parsley for garnish
¼ celery stick, finely diced

1. Sauté the diced onion in olive oil until golden.
2. Add crushed clove of garlic and sauté until also golden.
3. Add the tomato followed by the stock.
4. Bring all the ingredients to the boil, then reduce heat and simmer for 10 minutes.
5. Garnish with fresh parsley and the fined diced celery.

FOX FARM'S FISHY SOUP

I personally dislike most fish dishes. This soup is the only
way my poor wife can get me to eat any on a regular basis.

for the soup   **Serves 4 – 6**

1 large onion, peeled and thinly sliced
a pinch of saffron
30ml / 2 tablespoons of olive oil
2 tomatoes skinned, seeded and chopped
15ml / 1 tablespoon of tomato puree
1 litre / 1¾ pints of chicken stock
300ml / ½ pint of very dry white wine
1 bay leaf
the peel of 1 orange
1 celery stick, finely sliced
1 sprig of fresh fennel
1 teaspoon of tarragon, chopped
1 kg / 2¼ lb of mullet, haddock, plaice, turbot and cod, skinned and boned
100g / 4oz of peeled prawns
salt and freshly ground pepper
sliced brown bread, toasted gently

for the aioli (makes 150ml / ¼ pint)
2 large garlic cloves, crushed
1.25ml / ¼ teaspoon of light Dijon mustard
1 egg yolk
300ml / ½ pint of olive oil

1. Place the oil in a large pan, add the onions with a pinch of saffron and gently heat.
2. Stir in the tomatoes and tomato puree and simmer for a further 5 minutes.
3. Stir in the chicken stock, chopped celery and wine and bring to the boil until reduced.
4. Reduce the heat and add the bay leaf, orange peel, fennel, tarragon and salt and pepper.

5. Add the fish and simmer for 10–15 minutes, then add the prawns and continue cooking for 5 more minutes, or until all the fish is tender.

6. Season with salt and pepper and remove the bay leaf, orange peel and sprig of fennel prior to serving.

7. The ingredients for aioli should be mixed separately and served alongside the soup in a separate bowl with the toast.

TEXAN TOMATO SOUP

1 onion, finely chopped

1 celery stalk, finely sliced

1 tablespoon of olive oil

2 cloves of garlic, chopped

1 courgette, diced

1 X 400g / 14 oz can of sweet corn

1500ml / 2¼ pints of chicken stock

50 – 75g / 2–3oz of small dry pasta shells

4 large fresh tomatoes, diced finely

½ teaspoon each of dried basil, oregano and thyme leaves

1 teaspoon of salt

½ teaspoon of black pepper

½ teaspoon of sugar

50g / 2oz of grated Parmesan cheese

basil for garnish (optional)

Serves 6

1. Place the onion, celery, garlic and courgette into a pan with the olive oil and sauté contents until soft.

2. Add the sweetcorn and chicken stock. Bring to the boil and then add pasta and tomatoes.

3. Reduce the heat to a simmer for about 10 minutes, or until pasta is cooked.

4. Add seasonings.

5. Top each bowl with a sprinkling of parmesan cheese and a basil leaf just before serving.

POTAGER SOUP

All the veg listed here can be grown in a typical
allotment or vegetable plot. Luckily, we have such a plot.
If you or your better half are not adventurous with fruit
and veg then growing your own is a good way to
develop a taste. Without exception, whatever I have
grown to date I have enjoyed eating.

5ml / 1 teaspoon of vegetable oil   **Serves 6**
225g / 8oz of chopped broccoli
225g / 8oz of chopped carrots
1 stick of celery, sliced
1 large onion, sliced
800g / 1¾ lb of fresh, ripened chopped tomatoes
1 clove of garlic, chopped
1 litre / 1 ¾ pints of chicken stock
115g / 4oz of pasta, small shapes
2 tablespoons of grated parmesan cheese
parsley for garnish

1. Place the celery, onion and garlic in a pan with the oil and sauté until soft.
2. Add the pasta, broccoli, carrots, tomatoes and stock and simmer for a further
   15 minutes, or until the vegetables and pasta are cooked.
3. Season with salt and pepper.
4. Serve with parmesan and a sprig of parley as garnish.

COOL GARDEN SOUP

1 cucumber, peeled and sliced

1 green pepper, diced

1 small courgette, diced

250ml / 8 fl oz of tomato juice

4 large tomatoes, chopped and peeled

250ml / 8 fl oz of chicken stock

1 large onion, diced

the juice of 1 squeezed lemon

2 teaspoon of sugar

1 teaspoon of salt

a pinch of freshly ground pepper

Serves 4

1. Place the tomatoes, stock, onion, and green pepper in saucepan.
2. Bring contents to the boil and simmer for 20 minutes.
3. Cover to reduce evaporation.
4. Add the remaining ingredients, cover and simmer another 10 minutes.
5. Store in a fridge prior to serving and serve cold.

MINESTRONE SOUP

750ml / 1¾ pint of water   **Serves 8**

1 teaspoon of dried oregano

750ml / 1¾ pint of vegetable stock

2 cloves of garlic, crushed

400g / 14oz can of whole tomatoes, sliced

3 carrots, diced

1 celery stick, diced

1 onion, diced

½ courgette, diced

45ml / 3 tablespoons of red wine

1 large potato, diced

115g / 4oz of chopped parsley

180g / 6½oz tin of kidney beans

115g / 4oz pasta, small shapes

½ teaspoon salt and freshly ground pepper

1. Place the water, stock, tomatoes, carrots, celery, onion, wine, oregano, garlic, salt, and pepper in a saucepan.
2. Bring to the boil, then reduce the heat and simmer uncovered for about 40 minutes.
3. Add the courgette, beans, potatoes, parsley, and pasta.
4. Cook for about 20 minutes more.
5. Serve hot.

Snacks and Salads

SUMMER VEGETABLES

Even if you break into a cold sweat at the thought of cooking,
this is a beautifully simple addition that will put
sparkle into your main course.

1 small cauliflower, cut into florets

Serves 4

200g / 7oz of French beans
3 garlic cloves, crushed
2 carrots, thinly sliced
1 red pepper, sliced
500g / 1¼ lb of asparagus
30ml / 2 tablespoons of olive oil
15ml / 1 tablespoon of lemon juice
salt and freshly ground pepper

1. Cook the vegetables until still slightly crunchy.
2. Place in a large salad bowl and season with salt and pepper.
3. Mix the olive oil and lemon juice together and drizzle over the vegetables.
4. Serve immediately.

STUFFED TOMATO POTS

Tomatoes stuffed with anything always remind me of
my holidays in Greece when I was a medical student.
This particular recipe is much closer to home however –
it was actually suggested by a long-term patient and friend.

8 large fresh tomatoes   Serves 8
½ onion, diced finely
45ml / 3 tablespoons of lemon juice
1 teaspoon of finely chopped garlic
1 teaspoon of salt
¼ teaspoon of pepper
15ml / 1 tablespoon of olive oil
115g / 4oz of cooked rice
25g / 1oz of raisins

1. Cut a top slice off the stem end of the tomatoes and put aside – these can be used as the pot 'lids' later.
2. Scoop out the tomato centres. Discard the seeds, but dice any flesh removed and reserve.
3. Place the tomato shells on kitchen paper upside down and allow them to drain.
4. Soak the raisins in boiling water for about 20 minutes and drain prior to mixing with the onions and all other ingredients into the cooked rice.
5. Use to fill the tomato 'pots'.

TOMATO BREAD

375g / 13oz cups strong white flour

1 teaspoon of salt

10 ml / 2 teaspoons of easy-blend dried yeast

50g / 2oz of sundried tomatoes in oil

175ml / 6 fl oz of lukewarm water

70ml / 2½ fl oz skimmed milk or soya milk

75 ml / 5 tablespoons of lukewarm olive oil, plus extra for brushing

3 or 4 fresh basil leaves, torn not chopped

plain flour for dusting

1. Sift the flour into a large mixing bowl, then stir in the salt, yeast, tomatoes and torn basil leaves.
2. With your fingers, make a large dimple in the centre of the dry ingredients and pour in the water, milk and oil.
3. Mix until the ingredients make a soft dough then knead the dough on a lightly flour-dusted surface for about 10 minutes. Shape it into an oblong loaf.
4. Brush the top with oil, cover with clear film and leave to rise in a warm place for about 1 hour.
5. Pre-heat the oven to 220°C (425°F / Gas Mark 7). Remove the clear film and sprinkle the top of the loaf lightly with flour.
6. Bake for 30–40 minutes until golden brown. Leave in tin for 5 minutes to cool. Then turn out onto a wire rack. The loaf should sound hollow when tapped on the bottom. Serve warm.

BROCCOLI SALAD

225g / 8oz of broccoli, cut into small florets   Serve 4

½ red onion, chopped finely

125g / 4oz of low fat turkey bacon, grilled and cut into strips

a handful of sunflower seeds and raisins

50g of very low fat mayonnaise

15g / ½ oz of sugar

15ml / 1 tablespoon of apple cider vinegar

1. Mix the broccoli, red onion, bacon, seeds, and raisins in a large bowl.
2. Mix the mayonnaise, sugar, and vinegar together.
3. Add the mixture to the salad.
4. Mix well and serve.

MARINATED CARROT SALAD

450g / 1lb of carrots, peeled and sliced   Serves 4

1 red pepper, cut into strips

1 green pepper, cut into strips

1 yellow pepper, cut into strips

1 red onion, diced

2 large fresh, ripe tomatoes

30ml / 2 tablespoons of red wine vinegar

10ml / 2 teaspoons of Dijon mustard

15ml / 1 tablespoon of Worcestershire sauce

15ml / 1 tablespoon of olive oil

2 teaspoons of sugar

Salt and freshly ground black pepper

1. Blend the tomatoes, vinegar, mustard, Worcestershire sauce, olive oil, sugar, salt and pepper, in a food processor or liquidiser to make a marinade.
2. Steam the carrots until cooked, but still slightly tender.
3. Pour the marinade mixture over the carrots whilst they are still warm.
4. Stir in peppers and onion.
5. Store in a fridge overnight.
6. Season to taste just before serving.

SALAD NIÇOISE

675g / 1½ lb of peeled potatoes Serves 4

225g / 8 oz green beans (topped and tailed)

3 eggs, hard boiled

1 medium sized lettuce, separated, washed and dried

105ml / 7 tablespoons of French dressing

225g / 8oz small tomatoes, quartered

400g / 14oz of canned tuna steak

25 g / 1oz of canned anchovy fillets

2 teaspoons of capers

12 black olives

1. Boil potatoes for 20 minutes, or until tender. Drain and cool under running water.
2. Boil the green beans for 6 minutes.   Drain and cool under running water.
3. Chop the potatoes into bite sized chunks.
4. Shell and quarter the eggs.
5. Place the lettuce, potatoes, eggs, green beans and tomatoes in a salad bowl.
6. Pour the French dressing over and toss the salad.
7. Arrange the tuna over the salad mix.
8. Garnish with anchovies, olives and capers.
9. Season to taste and serve.

WARM CABBAGE

1 medium red cabbage, sliced thinly Serves 4

450g / 1lb Cox's eating apples, sliced thinly

45ml / 3 tablespoons of demerara sugar

90ml / 6 tablespoons of white wine vinegar

25g / 1oz of Flora margarine or soya – based margarine

1. Put all the ingredients in a large casserole dish.
2. Place in a low heat oven (150°C / 300°F / Gas Mark 2) for about 3 hours, stirring occasionally.
3. Season with salt and pepper.
4. Serve hot from the oven.

TUNA SALAD

Tuna is actually a very good source of non-meat protein
and Omega 3 fatty acids. It is an advantage that this is also so tasty!

175g / 6oz French beans   Serves 6
225g / 8oz tin of butter beans
225g / 8oz of tuna
2 celery sticks, sliced
1 onion, diced
150ml of French dressing
½ small cos lettuce
2 tomatoes, quartered
1 tablespoon of fresh parsley as garnish
salt and freshly ground black pepper

1. Boil the French beans in lightly salted boiling water for 10 minutes.
2. Drain and rinse well then cut the beans into small pieces.
3. Stir in the butter beans and tuna, celery and onion.
4. Pour over the French dressing.
5. Season to taste.
6. Toss lightly until all the ingredients are coated with the dressing.
7. Line the salad bowl with lettuce leaves arrange the tomatoes and mix inside.
8. Garnish with parsley.

RED CABBAGE AND GREEN APPLES

5 green apples

2 medium sized red cabbages

2 red onions

2 cloves of garlic, crushed

4 tablespoons of Flora or soya-based margarine

60 ml / 4 tablespoons of red wine

30 ml / 2 tablespoons of wine vinegar

1 cinnamon stick

2 tablespoons of sugar

½ teaspoon of nutmeg

1. Remove the core from each cabbage and slice thinly.
2. Peel and slice the onion.
3. Peel and crush the garlic.
4. Peel and core the apples, slicing them into small segments.
5. In a large saucepan over moderate heat, melt the Flora and sauté the onions and garlic until soft.
6. Add cabbage and apples, tossing until the cabbage is slightly wilted.
7. Stir in the red wine, vinegar, cinnamon stick and sugar.
8. Turn the heat down and allow to simmer with the lid slightly ajar for about 45 minutes or until the cabbage is tender.
9. Add the nutmeg.
10. Allow to cool before serving.

Main Courses

BROCCOLIED COLCANNON

A traditional meal served at Hallowe'en.
The original recipe has been adapted here
to use more cruciferous vegetables and
minimal saturated animal fat. **Serves 4**

2kg / 4½lbs of potatoes
50g / 2oz of chopped broccoli
1 bunch of kale or cabbage (about 675g / 1½lb)
6 sprigs of fresh thyme
50ml / 2fl oz of skimmed milk or soya milk
4 spring onions, chopped
3 cloves of garlic, chopped
50g / 2oz of Flora margarine or soya based butter substitute
salt and freshly ground black pepper
sprig of parsley for garnish

1. Peel the potatoes and cook in lightly salted water for about 15 minutes until tender.
2. While waiting for the potatoes, mix the milk with the thyme and garlic in a pan and simmer for 10 minutes.
3. Strain the milky mix, discarding the thyme and garlic.
4. Remove the cabbage / kale leaves from their stems using a sharp knife and chop finely.
5. Place them in a steamer with about 2cm of water, along with the broccoli, and steam until vegetables are tender and crisp.
6. Once the potatoes are ready, mash them with the garlic flavoured milk and stir in the cabbage / kale and chopped spring onions.
7. Season to taste with salt and freshly ground pepper.
8. Pile into an oven-proof dish and dot with Flora or soya margarine.
9. Place under a hot grill and brown the top.
10. Add parsley to garnish.

SAM'S CHICKEN AND TOMATO HOT-BALLS

This quick meal is a good source of protein and is
packed with lycopenes and lignans.
My son Sam doesn't care about the nutritional
content but loves the taste.

2 slices of wholemeal bread (crust removed)   **Serves 4**

30ml / 2 tablespoons of skimmed milk or soya milk

1 garlic clove crushed

2 × 225g / 8oz chicken breasts

350ml / 12 fl oz of chicken stock

400g / 14oz of ripe tomatoes

15ml / 1 tablespoon tomato puree

90g / 3½oz of easy cook brown rice

1 tablespoon of chopped fresh basil to garnish

1. Place the bread into a food processor to make breadcrumbs. Put these in a separate bowl and mix with milk, salt, pepper and garlic.
2. Place the chicken in the processor and chop into fine pieces. Add the breadcrumb mix and blend together.
3. Shape the mix into 12 – 16 small balls and chill in a fridge for at least 30 minutes.
4. Put stock, tomatoes and puree into a pan and bring to the boil.
5. Add the rice and turn down the heat to a simmer. Drop the chicken balls carefully into a pan and cook with the rice for about 15 minutes.
6. Stir the mix occasionally to ensure the rice does not stick to the pan and the chicken is cooked thoroughly and evenly.
7. Season with salt and freshly ground black pepper.
8. Serve hot.

TUNA STEAKS WITH ORANGE AND GRAPE SAUCE

For the soy sauce: **Serves 2**

> 1 teaspoon of cornflour
> 120ml / 4 fl oz of orange juice
> 1.25ml / ¼ teaspoon soy sauce

For the tuna:

> olive oil spray
> 2 handfuls of grapes (about 30)
> 2 × 110g / 4oz tuna steaks cut into strips
> 5ml / 1 teaspoon olive oil
> 120ml / 4 fl oz of orange juice
> 30ml / 2 tablespoons of lemon juice
> 50ml / 3 tablespoons of white wine
> a sprig of parsley

1. For the sauce, mix the cornflour, orange juice and soy sauce in a small pan.
2. Cook the sauce on a high heat for about a minute, stirring until it thickens.
3. Place the tuna steaks in a saucepan that has been lightly sprayed with cooking oil.
4. Using a juicer, liquidize about half the grapes and add their juice to the tuna.
5. Pour in the olive oil, orange juice, lemon juice, and wine.
6. Cook until just done, about 2–4 minutes on each side should do it.
7. Pour the sauce over the tuna prior to serving.
8. Garnish with parsley and the remainder of the grapes.

BAKED MACKEREL WITH PROVENÇAL SAUCE

2.5ml / ½ tablespoon of extra virgin olive oil   **Serves 4**

2 onions, sliced

4 medium size, thick mackerel fillets

6 olives, chopped

a sprig of parsley, chopped

a sprig of basil, chopped

1 tablespoon of capers

15ml / 1 tablespoon of balsamic or cider vinegar

4 medium sized tomatoes, chopped

1 stick of celery, sliced

2 cloves of garlic, crushed

salt and freshly ground pepper

1. Place mackerel fillets in a shallow baking dish.
2. Drizzle with olive oil and season with salt and pepper.
3. Combine all the other ingredients in a small bowl and pour over the fish.
4. Cover the dish with foil and bake in a pre-heated oven at 190°C (375°F / Gas Mark 5) for about 25 minutes.
5. Serve warm.

BROCCOLI AND MUSHROOM CASSEROLE

450g / 1lb of fresh broccoli   **Serves 6**

1 onion, diced

25g / 1oz of Flora or soya based margarine

2 cans of condensed cream of mushroom soup, low fat

25g / 1oz of grated blue cheese, low fat if possible

100g / 4oz instant rice

1. Steam the broccoli until tender.
2. Sauté the onions in margarine until soft.
3. Place the broccoli, onions and cheese in a large casserole dish.
4. Pour over the mushroom soup and stir in the rice.
5. Place in a pre-heated oven at 180°C (350°F / Gas Mark 4) for about 20 minutes.
6. Serve piping hot.

BROILED SALMON FILLET WITH WINE AND WATERCRESS SAUCE

For the wine sauce: **Serves 6**

200ml / 7 fl oz of chicken stock

75ml / 5 tablespoons of very dry white wine

1 spring onion, diced

50ml / 2 fl oz of skimmed milk or soya milk

2 teaspoons of cornflour

a handful of watercress

a sprig of parsley, chopped

1 bay leaf

For the salmon :

2 × 110g / ¼ lb salmon fillets

5ml / 1 teaspoon of olive oil

30ml / 2 tablespoons of lemon juice

salt and freshly ground pepper

For the wine sauce:

1. Mix chicken stock, wine, onions and bay leaf together in a small saucepan.
2. Bring to the boil then reduce heat to a simmer to allow the stock to reduce.
3. Remove the bay leaf.
4. In a separate small bowl, blend the milk (or soya milk) and cornflour with a small wire whisk until smooth.
5. Add milk mix to the stock mixture and slowly bring to the boil, stirring constantly to avoid lumps.
6. Continue to cook for about 1 minute and then pour the sauce into a blender and add watercress and parsley.
7. Blend to a smooth sauce.
8. Return sauce to saucepan and heat before serving.

For the salmon:

1. Brush the salmon with olive oil and sprinkle with lemon juice, salt and pepper.
2. Spray a pan with cooking oil, then place the salmon in the pan and grill for about 8 minutes.
3. Serve with lemon wedges and wine sauce.

JACK'S TOMATO CAPRESE

My middle son, Jack, likes this one.
He is the slowest eater in the East of England normally,
but manages to wolf this down in time for seconds.

4 large ripe tomatoes   **Serves 4**
220g / ½lb 'light' mozzarella
¼ cup fresh basil
30ml / 2 tablespoons extra-virgin olive oil
15ml / 1 tablespoon of white wine vinegar
1 teaspoon of Dijon mustard
¼ teaspoon mixed herbs

1. Slice the tomatoes and mozzarella into ¼ inch-thick slices.
2. Arrange the tomatoes, mozzarella and basil on a large serving dish, overlapping and alternating them.
3. For the dressing mix the olive oil, white wine vinegar, Dijon mustard and herbs. Drizzle the dressing over the salad.
4. Season to taste with salt and pepper.

SALMON PARCELS

4 × 115g / 4oz salmon fillets   **Serves 4**

10ml / 2 teaspoons of soy sauce

30ml / 2 tablespoons of dry sherry

1 tablespoon of fresh ginger, grated

2 garlic cloves, crushed

4 large savoy cabbage leaves

1 spring onion, finely chopped

1 tablespoon of chopped coriander

30ml / 2 tablespoons of lemon juice

1. Put the salmon fillets in a large dish.
2. Mix the soy sauce, sherry, ginger and garlic together and pour the mixture over the fish.
3. Cover the dish and allow to marinade in the fridge for at least half an hour.
4. Remove the salmon from marinade and place one fillet on each cabbage leaf in another large dish.
5. Place the spring onion and coriander in a small bowl and season with salt and pepper to taste.
6. Sprinkle each salmon fillet with ¼ of the onion mix.
7. Fold cabbage leaf over the salmon to create a parcel, holding the parcel in position with a small wooden cocktail stick.
8. Steam the parcel for about 20 minutes (or until both cabbage and salmon are tender).
9. Remove cocktail sticks before serving.

COURGETTE FETTUCCINE

450g / 1lb fettuccine pasta shapes
450g / 1lb can of tomatoes
30ml / 2 tablespoons of olive oil
½ onion chopped
4 slices pancetta chopped finely
1 courgette diced into small pieces
2 bay leaves
50ml / 2 fl oz white wine

Serves 4

1. Sauté the onion and pancetta in olive oil until golden brown then add chopped tomatoes, bay leaves and courgette.
2. Add the white wine and bring to the boil, simmering until contents are soft.
3. In a separate pan, cook the fettuccine until al dente.
4. Mix everything together.
5. Season with salt and freshly ground pepper.
6. Serve immediately.

COQ AU VIN

30ml / 2 tablespoons of olive oil   **Serves 4**

125g / 4oz of button mushrooms, left whole

25g / 1oz of Flora or soya-based margarine

1.6 kg / 3½ lb chicken cut into 8 pieces and skinned

115g / 4oz bacon cut into strips, with all fat removed

115g / 4oz button onions, peeled

2 garlic cloves, crushed

30ml / 2 tablespoons of brandy

250ml / 8 fl oz of red wine

300ml / ½ pint chicken stock

1 bouquet garni

25g / 1oz of Flora margarine or soya-based butter substitute, blended with 2 tablespoons of flour

salt and freshly ground black pepper

chopped parsley to garnish

1. Pre-heat the oven to 160°C (325°F / Gas Mark 3).
2. Heat the oil and margarine in a large frying pan and brown chicken pieces on all sides. Transfer into a casserole dish.
3. In the remaining margarine, heat the bacon strips, peeled onions, mushrooms and crushed garlic. Add to the casserole dish.
4. Add the brandy, red wine, stock, bouquet garni and seasoning to the casserole.
5. Cover and cook for about 1 hour in the pre-heated dish.
6. Remove the chicken, add the bouquet garni and keep warm.
7. Thicken the sauce with the margarine / flour mixture and season to taste.
8. Cook for several minutes and replace the chicken.
9. Sprinkle with parsley and serve.

LATE LUCKY PASTA

This is a good recipe when you are late home.

If you are late as often as I am you are lucky if you get any dinner!

100g / 6oz of fresh broccoli, broken into small florets   **Serves 4**

1 small onion, chopped finely

15 ml / 1 tablespoon of olive oil

25g / 1oz lean bacon, chopped into strips

1 pepper, sliced into small strips

1 × 400g, 14oz of canned tomatoes, chopped

1 teaspoon of sugar

125ml / ¼ pint vegetable stock

150g / 5oz of pasta

1. Put the onion, garlic, chopped bacon and peppers into a pan with olive oil. Sauté gently over a low heat. Add tomatoes and stock. Reduce slightly and remove from heat.

2. Meanwhile, in a separate pan, steam the broccoli until just tender and add to the tomato mixture.

3. Cook the pasta according to the packet instructions. Add broccoli and pour the tomato sauce over.

4. Serve immediately.

RAVIOLI À LA HOLLY

My little girl, Holly, is only 3 years old but has already developed a keen tooth for pasta. She really loves making pasta from scratch, albeit with a little help from her mum. It takes longer to scrape the pasta off the kitchen walls than it takes her to scrape it off her plate. This one is her favourite.

6 basil leaves, torn
6 large, ripe, tomatoes, chopped
200g / 7oz mozzarella, roughly chopped
10 slices of prosciutto, fat removed
450g / 1lb of sheets of fresh lasagne pasta
olive oil
50g / 2oz Parmesan cheese
salt and freshly ground black pepper

Serves 4

1. Mix the parmesan, basil, tomatoes and mozzarella in a bowl.
2. Stir together and season to taste.
3. Slice the prosciutto in half.
4. Place 1 heaped teaspoon of the filling mix at one end of a piece of prosciutto, roll up so that the filling is enclosed. Repeat this until you have used all the ingredients, making about 20 packages.
5. Using a serrated pasta cutter, cut pasta into 40 squares.
6. Place a prosciutto ball into a pasta square. Dampen edges with water and top with another pasta square. Press the edges together to seal. Repeat with remaining prosciutto balls.
7. Cook the filled ravioli in gently boiling salted water for about 3-4 minutes then drain.
8. Drizzle the olive oil over the packages and season to taste.
7. Garnish with the torn basil and serve.

KOFTAS IN TOMATO SAUCE

For the koftas
Serves 4

675g / 1½lb boneless chicken breasts or thighs

1 onion, grated

1 garlic clove, crushed

1 tablespoon chopped fresh parsley

1 tablespoon of fresh thyme

½ teaspoon ground cumin

½ teaspoon ground coriander

1 egg beaten

seasoned flour for rolling

50ml / 2 fl oz of olive oil

salt and pepper

basil leaves to garnish

For the tomato sauce

30ml / 2 tablespoons of olive oil

2 large onions, finely chopped

2 cloves of garlic, chopped

800g / 1¾lb of canned tomatoes, in their juice

basil and oregano seasoning (or use a herb of your choice)

½ teaspoon of harissa paste

60ml / 4 tablespoons of tomato puree

For the koftas:

1. Start by preheating your oven to 180°C (350°F / Gas Mark 4).
2. Chop the chicken into small pieces and place in a bowl with onion, garlic, herbs, spices and beaten egg. Once mixed, shape contents into small balls. Roll lightly in seasoned flour.
3. Brown the balls in oil in a frying pan, keeping the oil very hot.
4. Remove and drain on kitchen paper. Don't worry if they look a little under cooked, they will cook further in the sauce later.

For the sauce:

1. Sauté the onions, harissa and garlic in olive oil over gentle heat until the onion is transparent.
2. Chop the tomatoes and add to onions and garlic, along with juice from the tomatoes.
3. Add tomato puree and herbs.
4. Mix well and simmer gently for about 10 minutes.

Finally place the chicken balls in an ovenproof dish and cover with the sauce.
Cook in a pre – heated oven for 45 minutes.
Season with salt and pepper and garnish with a sprig of basil leaf.

CRUNCHY LEMON SARDINES WITH RICE

200g / 7oz wholegrain brown rice   **Serves 4**
8-12 medium fresh sardines, cleaned
zest and juice of 1 lemon
½ cucumber, roughly chopped
3 tomatoes, de-seeded and roughly chopped
1 small red onion, finely sliced
2 red skinned apples, cored and sliced
6 tablespoons of parsley, finely chopped
4 tablespoons of chopped fresh dill
2 tablespoons of almonds

1. Cook the rice until tender, drain and rinse under cold water.
2. Place sardines in a shallow dish and pour over half the lemon juice. Season with pepper and set aside.
3. Stir the vegetables, apples, herbs, zest and remaining juice into the rice, seasoning with black pepper.
4. Grill the fish for about 5–10 minutes, turning occasionally.
5. Serve with rice, salad and lemon wedges. Place the almonds on the surface of the fish (these look pretty and add a little crunch to the dish).

Desserts

CHILLED SUMMER FRUIT CHEESECAKE

For the crumb crust: **Serves 8**

    ½ packet of low fat digestive biscuits, crushed

    2 tablespoons of demerara sugar

    50g / 2oz of low fat spread

For the filling:

    275 g / 10oz low fat soft cheese or tofu soya substitute

    200 g / 7oz of low fat or soya yoghurt

    1 tablespoon powdered gelatin

    60 ml / 4 tablespoons of apple juice

For the topping:

    175 g / 6oz mixed summer soft fruit, e.g. strawberries, raspberries, redcurrants, blackberries

    2 tablespoons of redcurrant jelly

    30ml / 2 tablespoons of hot water

To make the crust:

1. Crush biscuits by placing in a plastic bag and rolling firmly with a rolling pin until you produce fine crumbs.

2. Melt the spread in a saucepan over gentle heat.

3. Stir in the biscuit crumbs and sugar.

4. Mix well and press into the base of the cake tin.

To make the filling:

5. Beat the yoghurt and soft cheese (or tofu) together with an electric whisk until smooth.

6. Dissolve the gelatin into the apple juice and then stir this mix into the tofu and yoghurt.

7. Spread the filling evenly over the crumb base and chill in a fridge for 4 hrs.

To make the topping:

8. Arrange the soft fruit on top of the cheesecake.

9. Melt the redcurrant jelly in a pan over a low heat, then add 2 tablespoons of hot water.

10. When cool, use to glaze fruit.

BAKED RASPBERRY CHEESECAKE

For the crumb crust: **Serves 8**

½ packet of low-fat digestive biscuits, crushed

2 tablespoons of demerara sugar

50g / 2 oz of low fat spread

For the filling:

900g / 2 lbs / 2 blocks of tofu

3 eggs

115g / 4oz sugar

5ml / 1 tablespoon of vanilla essence

For the topping:

2 teaspoons of cornflour, dissolved in 30ml / 2 tablespoons of hot water

50g / 2oz sugar

275g / 10oz fresh raspberries

To make the crust:

1. To crush the biscuits, place them in a plastic bag and roll over firmly with a rolling pin until they become fine crumbs.
2. Melt the spread in a saucepan over gentle heat.
3. Stir in the biscuit crumbs and sugar.
4. Mix well and press into the base of the cake tin.

To make the filling:

5. Place the tofu, eggs, sugar and vanilla essence in a blender and combine together until mix is a smooth thick cream.
6. Pour the mix into the tin on top of the crust and bake at 180°C (350°F / Gas Mark 4) for 30–45 mins, until firm to the touch.
7. When cool, place in a fridge for a couple of hours and allow to chill.

To make the topping:

8. Combine the raspberries and sugar in a saucepan over a low heat.
9. Add the cornflour paste and stir gently, so as not to 'pulp' the fruit.
10. When mix starts to turn syrupy, remove from the heat and allow to cool.
11. Pour over the top of the cheesecake just before serving.

MELON WITH SUMMER BERRIES

If you can get really fresh fruit, or better still grow your own,
this is a lovely summer dessert, stuffed with lycopenes,
Vitamin C and fructose.

175g / 6oz raspberries   **Serves 4**
175g /6oz strawberries
15ml / 1 tablespoon of icing sugar, sifted
45ml / 3 tablespoons of Grand Marnier (or orange juice)
2 Honeydew melons

1. Place the berries in a bowl with the icing sugar and liqueur (or orange juice).
2. Cut the melons in half, scoop out and discard the seeds.
3. Spoon the fruit into the melon halves.
4. Serve immediately.

WATERMELON AND GRAPE COMPOTE

1 small red watermelon   **Serves 6**
125 g / 4oz of seedless black grapes, halved
125 g / 4oz of seedless white grapes, halved
the juice of 1 lemon
25ml / 1½ tablespoons of honey
45 – 60ml / 3–4 tablespoons of Orange Curaçao
Mint sprigs to decorate

1. Quarter the watermelon, cut out the flesh and discard the seeds.
2. Place the melon in a bowl with the grapes.
3. Combine the lemon juice, honey and Curaçao, then pour over the fruit.
4. After about an hour, spoon into individual glass dishes and decorate with mint sprigs.
5. Serve immediately.

GUAVA SURPRISE

A tasty dessert rich in anti-oxidants.
If you value your front teeth you will make sure
all the guava pips are removed to avoid the surprise!   **Serves 6**

2 oranges
400g / 14oz of canned guavas
3 sliced bananas
125 g / 4oz halved and seeded black grapes,
2 passion fruit
5 or 6 sliced strawberries as garnish

1. Slice the guavas and keep their juice to one side. Remove their pips as you go.
2. Peel the oranges, removing all pith, and cut into segments. Halve the passion fruit and scoop out the fleshy portion. Place them all into a large bowl along with the sliced bananas and halved grapes.
3. Pour on the juice from the guavas.
4. Garnish with sliced strawberries.
5. Store in a cool refrigerator prior to serving. Can be served with low fat or soya yoghurt.

BOOZY STRAWBERRIES

675g / 1½lb of fresh strawberries   **Serves 4**
30ml / 2 tablespoons of caster sugar
Grated rind and juice of ½ orange
30ml / 2 tablespoons of either Cointreau or Grand Marnier

1. Divide 450g / 1lb of the strawberries between 4 individual serving dishes.
2. Place the remaining 225g / ½lb of strawberries in a bowl with the sugar and orange rind, then mash to a pulp using a fork.
3. Add the orange juice and liqueur and mix thoroughly.
4. Pour the pulped mixture over the whole strawberries (alternatively, if preferred, the pulped mixture can be pushed through a sieve to remove the pips, producing a smoother sauce).
5. Chill the mix in a fridge prior to serving.

Alternatively, substitute orange juice for the liqueur. It still tastes wonderful but looses a little of its kick and some of its boozy quality.

VANILLA PUDDING

100g / 4oz of sugar   **Serves 4**
45ml / 3 tablespoons of cornflour
a pinch of salt
500ml / 1 pint of skimmed milk or soya milk
10ml / 2 teaspoons of vanilla extract

1. Place the sugar, salt and cornflour in a saucepan.
2. Place over a low heat and slowly add the milk / soya milk, stirring constantly to prevent lumps from forming.
3. Bring to the boil, then reduce heat and simmer for about 5 minutes, stirring constantly until mixture is creamy and thick.
4. Remove from heat, stir in vanilla extract.
5. Pour the mix into dessert cups. Chill for several hours in a fridge until mixture sets.

Drinks

SAM'S STRAWBERRY AND APPLE SMOOTHIE

My youngest son, Sam, loves fruit – but he didn't always.
We found smoothies a great way of supplementing his intake.
There is no reason why you can't employ a similar approach
to introduce your better half to fruit if he is something of
a fruit heathen.
The soya milk may not sound good but in this format it is
disguised to such an extent that even traditional milk drinking
'carnivores' or kids can enjoy.

> *a handful of fresh strawberries*
> *2 eating apples*
> *30ml / 2 tablespoons of water*
> *a handful of crushed ice*
> *30ml / 2 tablespoons of skimmed milk or soya milk*

1. Mix ingredients in a blender.

RASPBERRY AND PEAR SMOOTHIE

> *a handful of fresh raspberries*
> *2 fresh pears*
> *30ml / 2 tablespoons of water*
> *a handful of crushed ice*
> *30ml / 2 tablespoons of skimmed milk or soya milk*

1. Mix ingredients in a blender.

APPLE AND APRICOT SMOOTHIE

1 large apple, peeled and cored
250ml / 8 fl oz apple juice
4 fresh apricots, stoned and peeled
1 banana, peeled
175ml / 6 fl oz low fat or soya-based yoghurt
10 ice cubes
15ml / 1 tablespoon of honey

1. Mix ingredients in a blender.

TOFU SMOOTHIE

150 ml / ¼ pint of soft tofu
a handful of strawberries
1 banana
105 ml / 7 fl oz of pineapple, orange or apple juice
2 ice cubes

1. Blend ingredients until smooth.

MIDSOMER FRUIT JUICE

2 apples
2 pears
1 large banana
1 cup of fresh raspberries
50ml / 2 fl oz of skimmed milk or soya milk

1. Blend ingredients until smooth.

STRAWBERRY AND BANANA DRINK

1 handful of fresh strawberries
600ml / 1 pint of skimmed milk or soya milk
1 ripe banana

1. Blend ingredients until smooth.

BANANA AND NUTMEG

1 banana
a pinch of grated nutmeg
175 ml / 6 fl oz of skimmed milk or soya milk

1. Blend ingredients until smooth.

RASPBERRY BANANA TOFU ICE POPS

a handful of either fresh or frozen raspberries
1 banana
250ml / 8 fl oz of freshly-squeezed orange juice
1 package of square tofu, medium firmness

1. Blend all the ingredients then store in a freezer for several hours prior to serving. The colder the better!

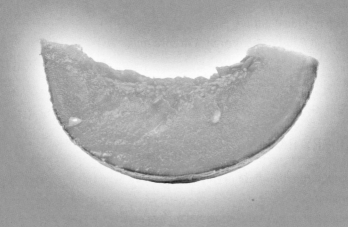

Juiced Fruit and Vegetables

These are a quick and easy way of increasing your dietary intake of fruit and vegetables. You lose a little of the fibre content by juicing (easily visible when you inspect the inside of the juicer machine). As a rule, try to avoid mixing fruit and vegetables together in drinks as you may suffer from excessive flatulence. You should probably restrict your intake to 2 or 3 glasses per day.

If you have diabetes keep a check on your diabetic control in case the natural sugar content in juiced fruit drinks upsets things. As a rule, do not peel the fruit first unless they are very thick skinned. Similarly don't remove the pips unless they are large. Juiced drinks are best diluted by 4 parts water / 1 part concoction first – this being especially true of green and red vegetable-based drinks.

JUICED FRUIT DRINKS

Try the following fruit in combination: oranges, pineapple, mango, strawberries, raspberries, passion fruit, grapefruit, plums or banana. As a rule, strawberries, apples and raspberries will mix well with most other fruit. Some examples are given below.

Try these fruit juices

2 slices pineapple + 1 mango

or

3 plums + ½ mango + ½ medium pineapple

or

3 guavas + 150g / 5oz raspberries + 1 peach

or

1 grapefruit + 1 mango + 1 passion fruit

or

4 tangerines + 125g / 4oz raspberries

or

1 apple + 1 peach + 1 mango

or

1 apple + 125g / 4oz blackberries + 125g / 4oz strawberries

JUICED VEGETABLES DRINKS

Not for the faint hearted, but are worth looking at.

Try these vegetable juices

Dilute 4 parts water / 1 part blend before drinking

75g / 3oz chunks of kale + 2 large carrots + 145ml / 5 fl oz water
or
2 large carrots + 4 broccoli florets + 4 cauliflower florets
or
125g / 4oz peas + 3 cabbage leaves + 2 large carrots + ½ parsnip
or
1 tomato + 1 stick celery + 2 large carrots + ½ lemon

USEFUL CONTACTS

PCaSO – Prostate Cancer Network
PO Box 66
Emsworth
Hampshire PO10 7ZP

0845 650 2555
www.pcaso.com

Cancer BACUP
3 Bath Place
Rivington Street
London EC2A 3JR
Freephone

0808 800 1234
www.bacup.org.uk

The Prostate Cancer Charity
3 Angel Walk
London W6 9HX

0845 300 8383
www.prostate-cancer.org.uk

CancerHelp UK
Institute for Cancer Studies
The University of Birmingham
Edgbaston, Birmingham B15 2TA

www.cancerhelp.org.uk

Macmillan Cancer Relief
Anchor House
15 – 19 Britten Street
London SW3 3TZ

0808 808 2020
www.macmillan.org.uk

Sexual Dysfunction Association
Windmill Place Business Centre
2 – 4 Windmill Lane
Southall, Middlesex UB2 4NJ

0870 774 3571
www.sda.uk.net

The Continence Foundation
307 Hatton Square
16 Baldwins Gardens
London EC1N 7RJ

0845 345 0165
www.continence-foundation.org.uk

Prostate Cancer Support Association (PSA)
Box 9434
London WC1N 3XX

0845 601 0766
www.prostatecancersupport.co.uk

SELECTED ARTICLES IN RECENT MEDICAL LITERATURE

Can diet affect prostate cancer?

Meyer J–P and Gillatt DA. *British Journal of Urology International* (2002), **89:** 250–254.

Vitamin E and prostate cancer.

Fleshner NE. *Urology Clinics of North America* (2002), **29:** 107–113.

Vitamin D and prostate cancer.

Konety BR and Getzenberg RH. *Urology Clinics of North America* (2002), **29:** 107–113.

The use of complementary / preventive medicine to prevent prostate cancer recurrence / progression following definitive therapy : Part I – lifestyle changes.

Moyad MA. *Current Opinion in Urology* (2003), **13:** 137–145.

The use of complementary / preventive medicine to prevent prostate cancer recurrence / progression following definitive therapy : Part II – rapid review of dietary supplements.

Moyad MA. *Current Opinion in Urology* (2003), **13:** 147–151.

Tomato products, lycopene and prostate cancer risk.

Miller EC, Giovannucci E, Erdman JW, Bahnson R, Schwartz SJ and Clinton SK. *Urology Clinics of North America* (2002), **29:** 89–93.

The role of soy phytoestrogens in prostate cancer.

Castle EP and Thrasher JB. *Urology Clinics of North America* (2002), **29:** 71–81

Prostate cancer and selenium

Nelson MA, Reid A, Duffield-Lillico AJ and Marshall JR. *Urology Clinics of North America* (2002), **29:** 67–70.

Green tea and prostate cancer.

Gupta S and Mukta H. *Urology Clinics of North America* (2002), **29:** 49–57.

NOTES

NOTES

NOTES

Eat your way to a healthier prostate

INDEX

Apple and apricot smoothie	**80**
Baked mackerel with provençal sauce	**62**
Baked raspberry cheesecake	**74**
Banana and nutmeg drink	**81**
Basic pizza topping	**38**
Basic tomato sauce	**37**
Boozy strawberries	**77**
Broccoli	
and carrots bathed in orange sauce	**39**
and mushroom casserole	**62**
salad	**54**
broccolied colcannon	**59**
late lucky pasta	**68**
Spanish broccoli	**36**
Brockley tomato soup	**44**
Broiled salmon fillet with wine and watercress sauce	**63**
Cabbage	
broccolied colcannon	**59**
red cabbage and green apples	**57**
warm cabbage	**55**
Carrots	
and broccoli bathed in orange sauce	**39**
with orange glaze	**38**
marinated carrot salad	**54**
Chicken	
coq au vin	**67**
koftas in tomato sauce	**70**
Sam's chicken and tomato hot-balls	**60**

Chilled summer fruit cheesecake 73
Cool garden soup 48
Coq au vin 67
Courgette fettucine 66
Crunchy lemon sardines with rice 71

Fish
    baked mackerel with provençal sauce 62
    broiled salmon fillet with wine and watercress sauce 63
    crunchy lemon sardines with rice 71
    Fox Farm's fishy soup 45
    salad niçoise 55
    salmon parcels 65
    tuna dill sandwich spread 40
    tuna salad 56
    tuna steaks with orange and grape sauce 61
    Fox Farm's fishy soup 45

Gazpacho 44
Guava surprise 76

Hot spinach salad dressing 40

Jack's tomato caprese 64
Juiced fruit drinks 83
Juiced vegetable drinks 84

Koftas in tomato sauce 70

Late lucky pasta 68

Marinated carrot salad 54
Melon with summer berries 75
Midsomer fruit juice 80
Minestrone soup 49

Pasta
 courgette fettucine **66**
 late lucky pasta **68**
 ravioli à la Holly **69**
Potager soup **47**

Raspberry
 and pear smoothie **79**
 banana tofu ice pops **81**
 vinaigrette **35**
Ravioli à la Holly **69**
Red cabbage and green apples **57**

Salad niçoise **55**
Salmon parcels **65**
Sam's chicken and tomato hot-balls **60**
Sam's strawberry and apple smoothie **79**
Spanish broccoli **36**
Spanish orange salad dressing **36**
Strawberry
 boozy strawberries **77**
 Sam's strawberry and apple smoothie **79**
 Spanish orange salad dressing **36**
 Strawberry and banana drink **81**
Stuffed tomato pots **52**
Summer vegetables **51**

Texan tomato soup **46**
Tofu smoothie **80**
Tomato
 basic tomato sauce **37**
 Brockley tomato soup **44**
 Jack's tomato caprese **64**
 koftas in tomato sauce **70**
 Sam's chicken and tomato hot-balls **60**
 stuffed tomato pots **52**

Texan tomato soup	**46**
and basil sauce	**37**
bread	**53**
vinaigrette	**35**
Tom's tomato soup	**43**
Tuna	
dill sandwich spread	**40**
salad	**56**
steaks with orange and grape sauce	**61**
Vanilla pudding	**77**
Warm cabbage	**55**
Watermelon and grape compote	**75**